☺ Early Learning
Sticker Activity
Numbers

priddy ☺ books
big ideas for little people

1
one

one big car

What color is the car?

2
two

two fluffy ducklings

What noise do ducklings make?

3
three

three little babies

Which baby is holding a book?

four juicy red fruits

Which fruit is not
a strawberry?

4 four

five tall
soldiers

Find the soldiers. Are they all the same?

5 five

six little shoes

Can you match the pairs?

6 six

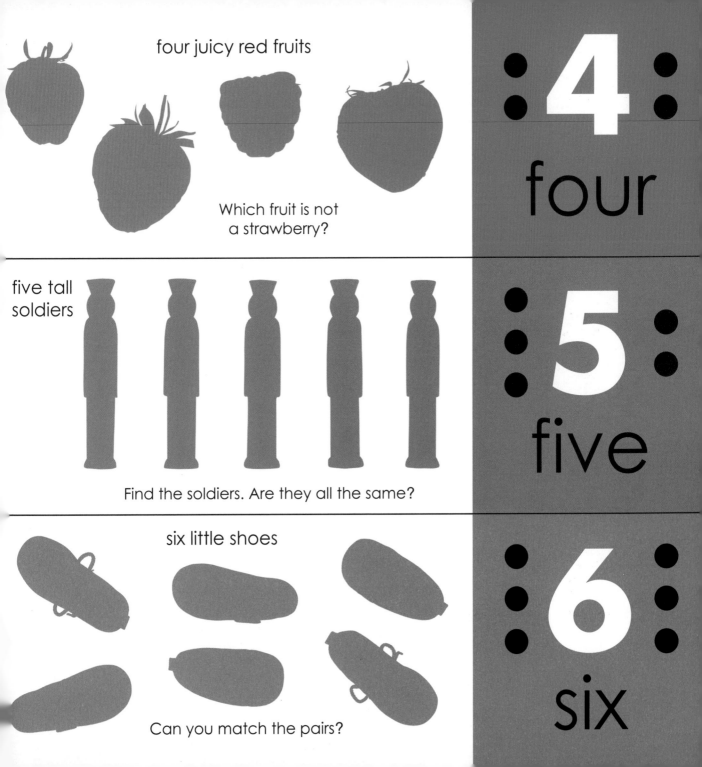

7

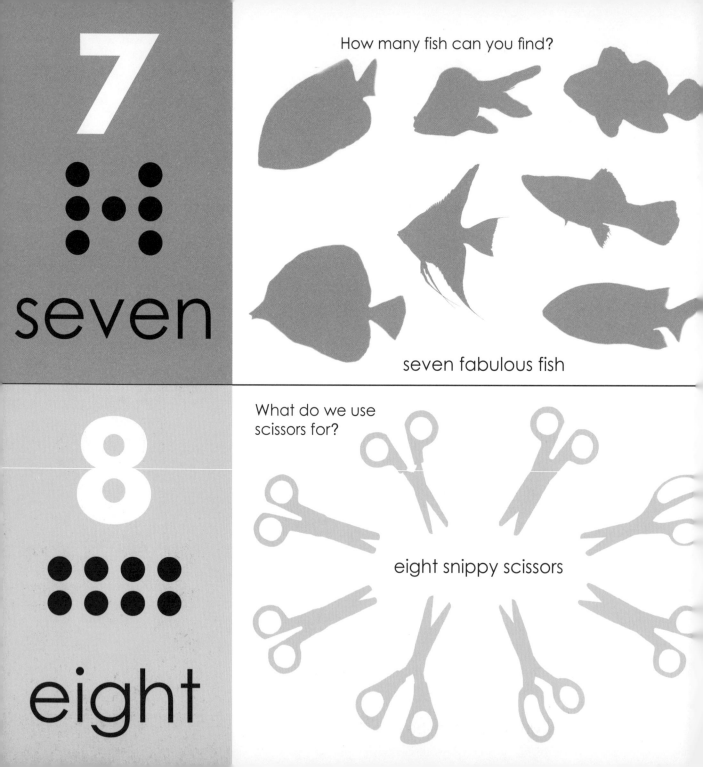

seven

How many fish can you find?

seven fabulous fish

8

eight

What do we use scissors for?

eight snippy scissors

Where do flowers grow?

nine beautiful flowers

9

nine

Which is the biggest star?

ten bright stars

10

ten

How many leaves?	**5**	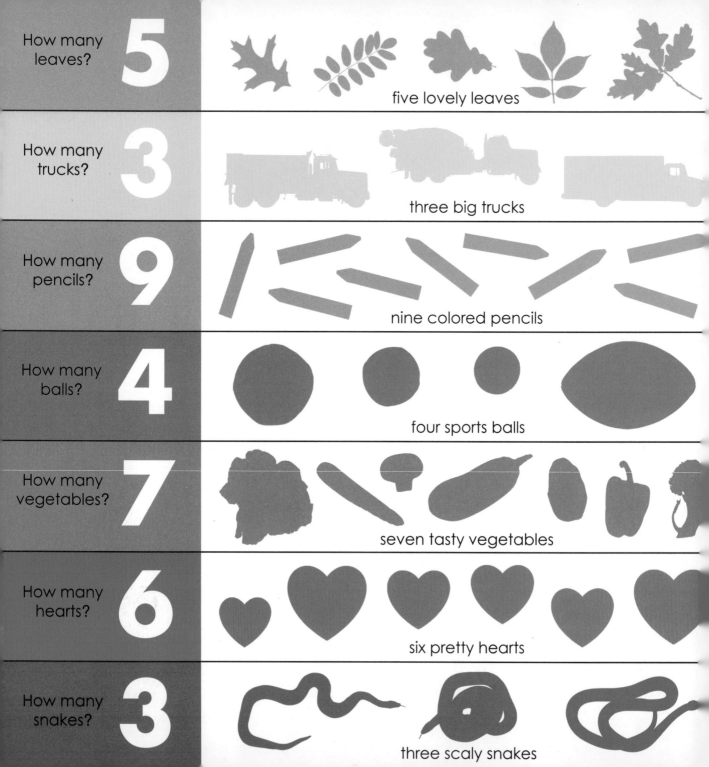five lovely leaves
How many trucks?	**3**	three big trucks
How many pencils?	**9**	nine colored pencils
How many balls?	**4**	four sports balls
How many vegetables?	**7**	seven tasty vegetables
How many hearts?	**6**	six pretty hearts
How many snakes?	**3**	three scaly snakes

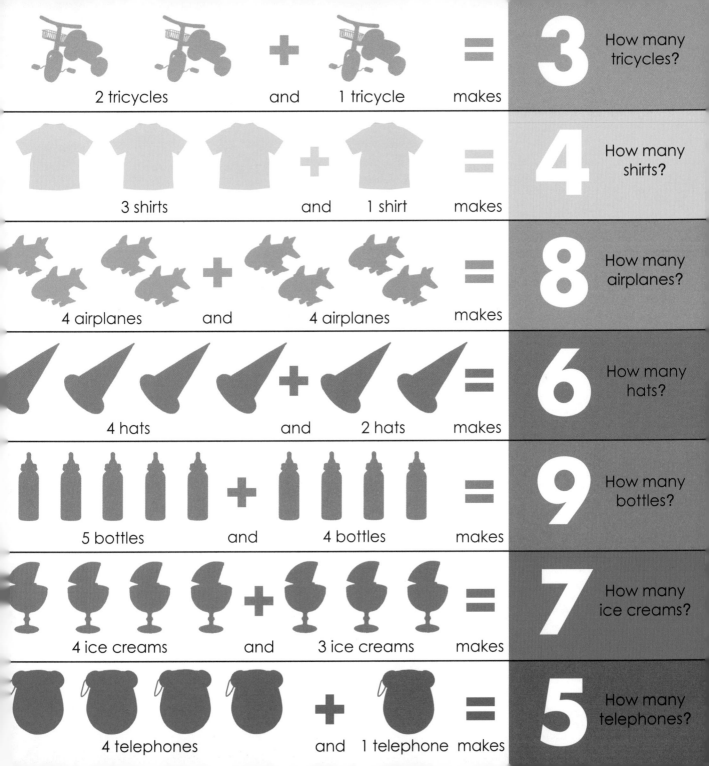

2 tricycles	and	1 tricycle	makes	**3** How many tricycles?
3 shirts	and	1 shirt	makes	**4** How many shirts?
4 airplanes	and	4 airplanes	makes	**8** How many airplanes?
4 hats	and	2 hats	makes	**6** How many hats?
5 bottles	and	4 bottles	makes	**9** How many bottles?
4 ice creams	and	3 ice creams	makes	**7** How many ice creams?
4 telephones	and	1 telephone	makes	**5** How many telephones?

How many clouds?

What is there one of?

Can you count the butterflies?

Are there more goats or pigs?

Can you count the pigs?

How many hens?

How many swans?

What are there two of?

Are there more ducklings or goldfish?

1

3

4

6

7

8

10

See if you can find out where these number stickers belong.

flower

telephone

soldier

fish

pencil

star

shoe

bottle

goldfish

shirt

heart

pencil

hat

duckling

goat

scissors

soldier

flower

tricycle

leaf

airplanes

scissors

pig

duckling

hat

fish

bottle

star

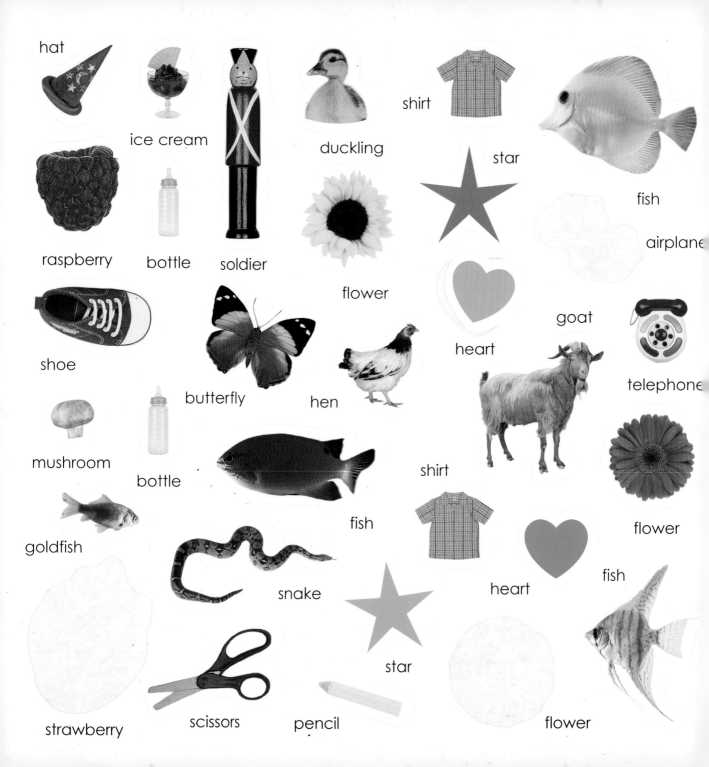

hat

ice cream

raspberry

bottle

soldier

duckling

shirt

star

fish

airplane

flower

heart

goat

telephone

shoe

butterfly

hen

mushroom

bottle

fish

shirt

flower

goldfish

snake

star

heart

fish

strawberry

scissors

pencil

flower

star

baby

flower

ice cream

scissors

broccoli

soldier

bottle

truck

butterfly

scissors

shoe

tricycle

heart

shoe

hat

leaf

fish

shoe

hen

star

star

airplanes

ball

pencil

fish

pencil

truck

duckling

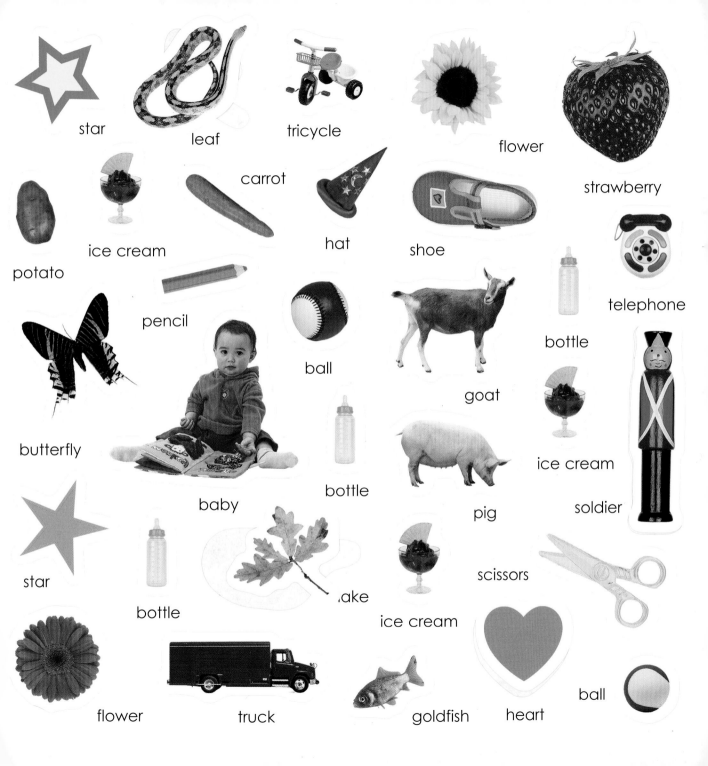

star

leaf

tricycle

flower

strawberry

carrot

ice cream

hat

shoe

telephone

potato

pencil

bottle

ball

goat

bottle

butterfly

baby

bottle

pig

ice cream

soldier

star

scissors

bottle

ake

ice cream

flower

truck

goldfish

heart

ball

strawberry

scissors

car

telephone

airplanes

leaf

leaf

eggplant

ball

ice cream

pencil

flower

hat

baby

goldfish

pencil

telephone

scissors

pencil

shirt

snake

pepper

bottle

shoe

heart

wan

lettuce

ice cream

scissors

star

1 one elephant

2 two shoes

3 three boats

4 four dinosaurs

5 five pigs

 six trains

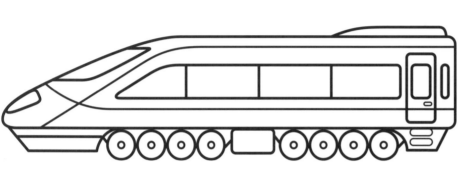

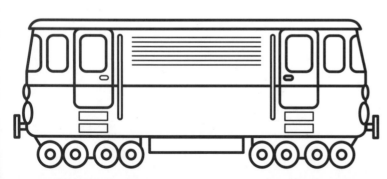

7 seven cupcakes

8 eight airplanes

 **nine ducks**

10 ten beach balls

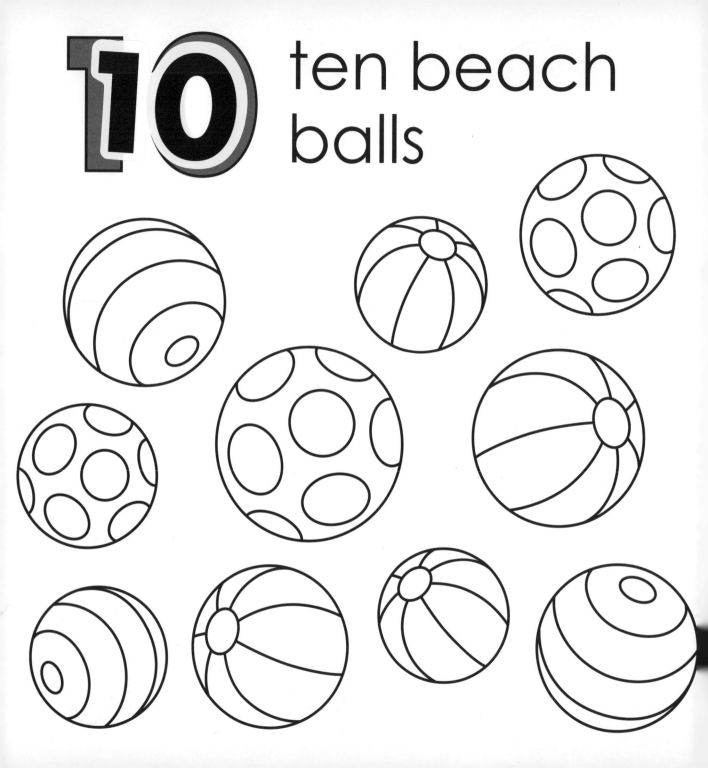

20 twenty flowers

Draw your own picture here

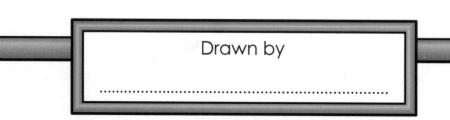

Drawn by

....